Halo the series

season 2 movie

preview

A guide revealing the

upcoming action-adventure

television series, including the

cast, plot details, release date

and everything you want to

Know

Paul B. Snyder

Table of contents

Introduction

An Extensive Analysis of Season 1 of "Halo"

The "Halo" series is one notable example of how video game adaptations have gained great traction in the realm of television and streaming platforms. This investigation explores the world of "Halo," a property that began as a ground-breaking video game series and has now made a successful and contentious transfer to television. We'll explore the spirit of "Halo" and analyze the successes and setbacks of Season 1 as we set out on this trip.

A Synopsis of the "Halo" Series

A sci-fi military franchise called "Halo," developed by Bungie and subsequently by 343 Industries, made its gaming debut in 2001 with the release of "Halo: Combat Evolved." The series chronicles the exploits of Master Chief, a supersoldier, as he faces off against the alien Covenant and other foes in a far-off future.

The intricate storyline, compelling gameplay, and well-known characters of the game swiftly made "Halo" a global phenomenon. Its popularity spread beyond video games to include novels, comic books, and even a future television series. The

"Halo" universe expanded into a vast story that captivated gamers all around the world.

An Overview of Season 1's Success and Controversies

Expectations were high when Paramount+ decided to take on the challenging challenge of adapting "Halo" for the tiny screen. With a highly anticipated debut, Season 1 was able to maintain its position as the most viewed program on the streaming service. By introducing viewers to the graphically gorgeous world of Xbox games, the series garnered remarkable popularity.

But success also brought controversy. The departure from the games' established storyline was one of the main sources of disagreement among fans. Enthusiasts of the video game "Halo" voiced their displeasure with the developers' choice to deviate from the plot and remove sequences in which Pablo Schreiber's character, Master Chief, shows his face. Fans felt betrayed by the artistic decisions chosen for the series, which led to outcry and contentious debates on social media.

The representation of Cortana, Master Chief's AI partner, was another divisive choice. The debate didn't end there. Divergent opinions among fans over the character's path resulted in contentious discussions on social media. Reviewers gave Season 1 positive scores despite these problems, demonstrating the difficult balancing act between appeasing ardent fans and drawing in new viewers.

Even though it was still in its infancy as a streaming service, Paramount saw the potential goldmine in the "Halo" franchise. The network's faith in "Halo"'s popularity and future on the small screen was evident in its decision to greenlight a second season before the first episode aired. Fan backlash and mistrust, however, greeted this decision as supporters believed their grievances from Season 1 were not being sufficiently addressed.

The "Halo" series has become a hot subject of conversation among its community as we go from the controversy of Season 1 to the excitement of Season 2. Fans have praised and discussed the series because of its unique perspective on known mythos and willingness to take chances. We'll go over all there is to know about Season 2 in the parts that follow, including the cast, teasers, anticipated story points, and the behind-the-scenes crew influencing "Halo"'s future on television.

Chapter 1

Behind the Scenes

Introducing "Halo" Season 2 Creators

Any television show's enchantment is a result of the committed work and inventiveness of the crew behind the scenes as much as the performers' on-screen antics. We will learn more about the production crew and the new showrunners who have taken over as we take a behind-the-scenes look at "Halo" Season 2. We'll also go deep into exclusive conversations with major players to get a personal look at their involvement in the much-awaited return of the show.

Insight into the Production Team and New Showrunners

Any TV show's ability to succeed often depends on the creativity and know-how of its production crew. A significant new face on the leadership team for "Halo" Season 2 is David Wiener, an Emmy-nominated producer best known for his work on "Fear the Walking Dead." Wiener's arrival infuses the "Halo" universe with new life and inventive energy, and fans can't wait to see how his influence plays out on the show.

The choice made by the program to hire new showrunners is a calculated attempt to advance the story and resolve any issues brought up in Season 1. Wiener, who has experience with character development, storyline dynamics, and overall production, promises a Season 2 that pays homage to the core of "Halo" while introducing fresh features that will engage viewers.

Actors Pablo Schreiber and Natascha McElhone have become executive producers for the first time, marking another change in the executive producing team. As seasoned actors within the series, their dual roles offer a unique blend of on-screen talent and behind-the-scenes influence, ensuring a symbiotic relationship between the characters and the overall storytelling direction. This change not only highlights their commitment to the series but also positions them as integral contributors to the creative decisions shaping the narrative of "Halo."

The "Halo" Season 2 producers are still major players in the business. Amblin Television continues to direct the production under the direction of industry veterans Steven Spielberg, Darryl Frank, and Justin Falvey. Under the direction of Frank O'Connor and Bonnie Ross, 343 Industries is still lending its experience to make sure the series remains loyal to its video game origins. Furthermore, One Big Picture, led by Otto Bathurst and Toby Leslie, continues to be an integral member of the production crew, contributing their unique perspective to the series.

The combination of these imaginative brains creates the foundation for a Season 2 that promises novelty while maintaining the essential components that have made the "Halo" series so popular.

Interviews with Key Cast Members about their Roles in Season 2:

Turning to the people who give life to the characters in "Halo" Season 2 is the only way to fully comprehend the core of the show. Key cast members' exclusive interviews provide a distinct perspective on their jobs, the difficulties they've experienced, and the anticipation for the next season.

Returning to the role of Master Chief, Pablo Schreiber provides insights into the development of his persona. Schreiber's choice to become an executive producer places an additional burden on her shoulders since she not only plays the legendary supersoldier on screen but also plays a part in the overall storyline. Interviews reveal that Schreiber is excited about the new path Season 2 is taking, promising viewers that future episodes would explore Master Chief's mental state and the fallout from Cortana's control.

In Season 2, Natascha McElhone, who portrays Dr. Catherine Halsey, discusses the nuances of her character's job. One important character in the "Halo" mythology who might have a big impact on the main story is the mysterious Dr. Halsey. McElhone's simultaneous job as executive producer highlights the show's collaborative aspect, as the performers actively participate in the creative choices that shape the plot.

Shabana Azmi, Natasha Culzac, and Yerin Ha are newcomers to the "Halo" world who provide new insights on their characters and the difficulties of entering a well-established series. Their interviews provide a window into the set camaraderie, the thrill of being a part of a famous series, and the commitment needed to live up to the expectations of new and old fans alike.

The interviews also touch on the Season 2 themes, such as the Covenant's imminent danger and the investigation of Forerunner relics. The character of Vannak-134, played by Bentley Kalu, makes references to the complex bonds between Spartans as well as the difficulties they would encounter in the next season.

These interviews give the larger-than-life "Halo" world a human touch as fans eagerly await the return of their beloved characters and the introduction of new faces. They act as a link between the passionate people who bring each storyline to life and the fantastical narrative playing out on screen.

Chapter 2

Character profiles

"Halo" Season 2's Vital Heart

The characters are the main characters in the vast "Halo" world; they weave together the complex story that has held viewers' attention for years. We'll go into the depths of the characters' personalities and look at how they change from the events of Season 1 to the much-awaited Season 2, as we undertake a thorough examination of the primary characters—with a special emphasis on the legendary Master Chief.

Master Chief - The Unyielding Protagonist

Pablo Schreiber's character Master Chief is the epitome of the "Halo" series. Wearing the recognizable Mjolnir armor, he is a supersoldier who has led the series from the start. We saw Master Chief's steadfast determination to foil the Covenant menace and his unflinching loyalty to the United Nations Space Command (UNSC) in Season 1.

Master Chief is going to have a lot of character development as we get into Season 2. Interviews with Schreiber demonstrate his dedication to examining the psychological makeup of this renowned character and the fallout from Cortana's takeover after Season 1. Schreiber's choice to become an executive producer highlights the collaborative process involved in creating Master Chief's journey, while also cementing his relationship with the character.

A more complex picture of Master Chief's development in Season 2 is anticipated, one that highlights the inner struggles resulting from his team's changed dynamics and the Covenant's impending danger. The storyline alludes to a Master Chief who must face personal struggles in addition to his duty to protect mankind from an imminent threat.

Dr. Catherine Halsey: The Mastermind Behind Fate

The way Natascha McElhone plays Dr. Catherine Halsey gives the "Halo" series a deeper level of nuance. Dr. Halsey, the clever brains behind the Spartan program, is crucial in determining the fate of characters such as Master Chief. Her persona in Season 1 was mysterious, motivated by a sense of purpose that went beyond the confrontations with the Covenant.

A deeper exploration of Dr. Halsey's intentions and the fallout from her actions is promised in Season 2. As the investigation of Forerunner relics and the approaching danger raises the stakes, the character's development takes center stage. An interesting element is added by McElhone's simultaneous status as executive producer, which implies a team effort to make sure Dr. Halsey's plotline flows well with the larger plot.

When Dr. Halsey's intelligence is contrasted with the events of Season 2, it becomes clear that she is a character who is considering moral quandaries and the possible consequences of her previous choices. Dr. Halsey is positioned as a character whose journey holds the key to deciphering deeper levels of the "Halo" story via the complex dance between science and morality.

Cortana: The Quiet Force Behind History

Cortana, Master Chief's AI companion, is portrayed by Jen Taylor, who brings a distinct dynamic to the show. Cortana played a crucial part in Season 1, daring to change the direction of the fight by taking control of Master Chief's body. In addition to upending the story's fundamental assumptions, this choice left viewers excitedly awaiting Season 2's outcomes.

Cortana's development becomes a key source of mystery as she becomes the silent force behind Master Chief's fate. The character's shift from friend to perhaps antagonistic force gives the story a degree of uncertainty. Interviews with Taylor allude to the difficulties Cortana would face, posing issues with identity, loyalty, and the fuzziness of the boundaries between humans and artificial intelligence.

With a deep examination of the character's internal conflicts and exterior effects on the overall story, Season 2 promises to reveal the fallout from Cortana's activities. The future of Master Chief and the whole "Halo" world might be determined by the silent driver.

Novel Individuals in the Spartan Hierarchy - Novel Views:

In Season 2, new Spartans join the fight, each contributing a unique set of skills and viewpoints to the group. The Spartan squad benefits from new dynamics provided by characters like Kwan Ha (Yerin Ha),

Vannak-134 (Bentley Kalu), and Riz-028 (Natasha Culzac). Their addition promises to provide fresh vitality to the series while also broadening the cast of characters.

The character of Riz-028 (Natasha Culzac) gives the squad an air of mystery. Her Spartan persona alludes to the many histories and origins that are interwoven throughout the UNSC. The Vannak-134 from Bentley Kalu is expected to provide a seasoned warrior's viewpoint and enhance the Spartan brotherhood. The way that Yerin Ha plays Kwan Ha adds a personal touch and gives the intergalactic conflicts a familiar grounding.

Observing the development of these new Spartans from Season 1 to Season 2 will be an interesting narrative thread. The way they work with the current squad, overcome Covenant obstacles, and advance the main plot will determine how the "Halo" series develops in the future.

Chapter 3

The Debates

Examining the Story Decisions in "Halo" Season 1

In the entertainment industry, debates on well-loved franchises often include controversial elements. Season 1 of "Halo," a show that has prospered due to its rich gaming heritage, but not without controversy. This investigation goes deep into the examination of the issues that sparked passionate discussions among enthusiasts, focusing on the departures from the game's narrative and the bold choice to hide Master Chief's face.

Deviations from the Game Storyline

A Rift in Lore:

The fact that "Halo" deviated from the game's established plot in Season 1 was one of the main points of discontent among the fan community. Enthusiastic gamers, who had devoted several hours to the rich and complex world of the games, were confronted with a storyline that changed course without warning. The decision to depart from the painstakingly created game narrative became the center of contentious debates on many social media sites.

The science fiction narrative standard was raised by the "Halo" games, which were renowned for their complex storylines and well-rounded characters. Fans responded passionately to Season 1's determination to forge its path by adding new features and breaking traditional narrative norms. While some thought it was a novel approach that would enable the show to give well-known characters new life, others felt it was a betrayal of the original material, which had amassed a sizable and devoted following over the years.

It's critical to comprehend the fine balance that modifications must achieve to analyze these disputes. On the one hand, artistic license may give a well-known world new life and startle even readers who are well-versed in the original work. However, going too far in one direction runs the danger of offending the same fans who first brought the brand to popularity. Season 1 of "Halo" finds itself at the crossroads of these ideas, sparking a conversation about the fine art of adaptation.

The Mystery Around Master Chief's Face Revealed

Throughout the "Halo" video game series, the choice to conceal Master Chief's face has remained unwavering. The famous hero, whose face was always hidden under the recognizable green helmet, came to represent secrecy and mystery. The mystery surrounding Master Chief had become second nature to fans, who now found it intriguing to learn his face.

But Season 1 decided to break with this long-standing custom. The bold decision to reveal Master Chief's face—or lack thereof—sparked a firestorm of criticism. The story option presented to fans who had been waiting impatiently for a peek beneath the helmet was unexpected. The choice called into question the value of preserving certain aspects of mystery in the narrative in addition to upending the foundations of accepted tradition.

The Reaction of Fans

A Melody of Unhappiness

The debates around "Halo" Season 1 went beyond internet forums and resulted in a chorus of negative feedback from fans. Forums, fan networks, and social media sites have become passionate battlegrounds for divergent points of view. Fans expressed their displeasure by pointing out apparent flaws and deviations from the established canon, arguing that the series had deviated too much from the games.

A portion of the fandom expressed strong disapproval of the choice to deviate from the game's plot and display Master Chief's face. Some believed that in order to appeal to a wider audience, the complex narrative that characterized the games had been abandoned and the spirit of "Halo" had been watered down. These criticisms often included yearning for the stories from the first games, indicating a desire for the franchise to stay true to its origins.

On the other hand, among the complaints there were many who valued the chances the authors had taken. They saw Season 1 as a chance to release "Halo" from the confines of well-established gaming mythology and present the series to a wider audience. These viewers applauded the series' courage to forge its own route and discover uncharted territory in the "Halo" world.

Paramount remained firm in its decision to greenlight a second season even before Season 1 had concluded, indicating a belief in the potential longevity and success of the series. The creators and the network showed resilience in navigating the fan backlash and sticking to the vision for "Halo." Even if it was strong, the debate proved how devoted fans are to the "Halo" world.

Keeping a Balance

Determining the Path for Season 2:

The upcoming release of Season 2 presents a chance for the series to address fan concerns and expand upon the foundations set in the first chapter, particularly in light of the ongoing debate surrounding Season 1 among the "Halo" community. With newfound knowledge from the discussions generated by Season 1, the producers must now do a careful balancing act.

It becomes clear by examining these disputes that "Halo" Season 2 is at a turning point. Even if they were contentious, the departures from the game canon could have created opportunities for original narrative. Despite being controversial, the choice to hide Master Chief's face has preserved the character's mystery. The second season serves as a canvas for the writers to hone their narrative decisions and address audience feedback while maintaining the series' signature creative audacity.

Rather than being a barrier, the criticisms surrounding Season 1 may be seen as a driving force toward development and adaptation. They provide insightful information on the complexities of bringing a popular video game series to television, where conflicting expectations must be carefully weighed against the need for creative storytelling.

In conclusion, the debates around "Halo" Season 1 have become essential parts of the show's continuing story, regardless of whether they are based on decisions about Master Chief's appearance or on departures from game history. The writers are in charge of an interplanetary story where the demands of a devoted fandom collide with the difficulties of adaptation as Season 2 is ready to premiere. The real test of "Halo's" fortitude and artistic vision is shown in this delicate dance, indicating that Season 2 will not only take lessons from the scandals of its predecessor but also seize the chance for improvement and atonement.

Chapter 4

Trailer Analysis

Revealing the Mysteries of "Halo" Season Two

We explore the nuances of both the first look and full trailers for Season 2, breaking down the visual cues, character glimpses, and narrative hints that have enthralled the fan community. Trailers are tantalizing glimpses that fan the flames of anticipation by offering a taste of what lies ahead in the expansive universe of "Halo." We also discuss the conjectures and fan ideas that have surfaced, creating a complex and fascinating web for the next season.

First Look Trailer

Introducing the Front Line of Combat

An epic cosmic battle is set in motion in the first look teaser, which was released on December 2, 2023, during the CCXP panel devoted to "Halo" Season 2. The 90-second teaser begins with a visual extravaganza of spaceships engaged in combat throughout the vast cosmos. The "Halo" series' eerie music emphasizes the seriousness of the approaching conflict.

The continuous conflict between the United Nations Security Council and the Covenant is one of the main story strands that is underlined in the first look. The war, which was the main focus of Season 1, seems to be getting worse, giving spectators hope for an action-packed season full of interplanetary conflicts.

The initial look's presence of important personalities is another significant feature. Master Chief, played by Pablo Schreiber, commands attention and radiates resolve and tenacity. Brief cameos by Shabana Azmi as Admiral Margaret Parangosky, Natasha Culzac as Riz-028, and Olive Gray as Dr. Miranda Keyes allude to their respective roles in the drama that is developing. The characters' fleeting appearances heighten the suspense and make viewers want to see how their stories develop.

With its crucial significance in Season 1, the enigmatic Forerunner relic is perhaps one of the most intriguing images in the first look. With its throbbing energy and mysterious meaning, the relic starts to represent both imminent disaster and possible redemption. Its presence in the teaser implies that Season 2 will still be fueled by the pursuit of Forerunner technology.

Full Trailer

January 11, 2024 - A Deeper Dive into Chaos

On January 11, 2024, the entire teaser was unveiled, giving audiences a closer look at the mayhem and mystery that will be revealed in Season 2. The visual extravaganza, which lasts the whole length of the video, combines tension, emotion, and jaw-dropping action scenes.

The aftermath of a horrific incident on a barren planet is one of the main themes that become apparent after watching the whole movie. Pablo Schreiber's character, Master Chief, struggles with the fallout from this incident and alludes to a storyline that explores the psychological cost of war. The teaser in the film suggests that this will be a turning point in the war, requiring the Master Chief to face not only outside enemies but also his own inner demons

The eerie narration, which may be Master Chief's, adds to the trailer's overall emotional impact. The monologue gives viewers a deeper level of reflection by revealing some of the renowned supersoldier's inner conflicts. With this narrative decision, Master Chief's austere and sometimes quiet persona from the video games is broken, allowing for a closer relationship with the character.

The revelation that the Covenant is getting ready to assault the biggest fortress mankind has ever had raises the stakes as the teaser goes on. It becomes evident how urgent the issue is, and Master Chief must risk everything to demonstrate the impending peril that others could overlook.

One of the main plot threads is the search for the Halo, which is said to contain the key to either humanity's survival or annihilation. The plot gains grandeur from the visual depiction of the Halo, a celestial ring hovering in space. This mission places the Halo at the center of the continuing struggle between the UNSC and the Covenant in addition to having connections to the Forerunner relics.

Fan Theories and Speculations

Cracking the Mystery

Following the release of the first look and complete trailers for "Halo" Season 2, fans began to conjecture and analyze every frame of the movie in an attempt to uncover plot twists and hidden hints.

A common conjecture is on the enigmatic and barren planet seen in the trailers. Supporters think that this planet may be connected to the startling incident that alters Master Chief's viewpoint. The nature of this incident is still unknown, with fans speculating about everything from a catastrophic Covenant strike to the possible discovery of a brand-new, powerful foe.

Excessive conjecture also surrounds the position of Cortana, Master Chief's AI partner. The character Cortana is now the quiet force behind Master Chief's fate, suggesting that she will continue to have an impact according to the teasers. Viewers speculate about what could happen as a result of Cortana's activities in Season 1, wondering how much power she really has and if it would affect Master Chief's choices.

There have been speculations on the meaning of the mysterious Forerunner artifact from Season 2, which is a visual highlight in the trailers. There are enthusiasts who believe the item might be the key to revealing the origins of the Halo rings or perhaps unlocking new technology. The artifact's cosmic iconography lends it an ethereal feel that encourages viewers to consider its significance to the overall story.

There is still a lot of debate on who is narrating the whole video. Enthusiasts are arguing passionately about who the voice belongs to—Master Chief, a brand-new character, or perhaps Cortana. Fans are anxious to peel back the layers of this narrative technique since the inclusion of a contemplative and poignant monologue implies a deeper investigation of the character's mind.

Although it was established in Season 1, the main topic of the UNSC-Covenant battle raises questions about possible friendships and betrayals in Season 2. Some fans speculate that Spartans and Covenant commanders may have to form unorthodox partnerships in order to fight a shared foe due to the Covenant's growing menace. The intergalactic battle is made more difficult by the possibility of internal turmoil among both camps.

Finally, the "Halo" Season 2 teasers act as a spark for fan speculation and excitement. In addition to conceptual subtleties and narrative allusions, the visual feast has sparked a passion among fans. With each passing frame, fans are delving deeper into their elaborate ideas and trying to solve the mystery surrounding the forthcoming episode as the season debut approaches. The teasers have not only piqued interest in the upcoming "Halo" film but have also sparked excitement among the general public about the upcoming cosmic odyssey.

Chapter 5

Recap of Season1

"Halo's Cosmic Tapestry"

"Halo"'s first season thrust viewers into the center of an intergalactic war while balancing the game series' well-known lore with novel character development and twists. This in-depth synopsis endeavors to dissect the pivotal moments and narrative threads that characterized the first season, exploring the ramifications of Cortana assuming command of Master Chief's physique—a transformative development that left fans excitedly awaiting the repercussions in Season 2.

The Galactic Battlefield

United Nations Space Command vs. The Covenant

Season 1 is set against the backdrop of a galaxy engulfed in an unending war. The bold Master Chief (Pablo Schreiber) of the United Nations Space Command (UNSC) takes on the powerful Covenant, an extraterrestrial coalition out to rule the universe. The Covenant's invasion of the rebel planet Madrigal ignites the conflict, which sets up a sequence of titanic fights and calculated moves.

Kwan Ha (Yerin Ha), a young survivor of the Covenant's attack on Madrigal, is the main character of the story. After Kwan is saved by a group of super-warriors known as the Spartans, who are commanded by Master Chief, he becomes a key figure in the ongoing fight for independence and a symbol of the human rebellion against the Covenant.

Forerunner Artifacts and The Covenant's Pursuit:

A Catalyst for Conflict

In Season 1, the finding of Forerunner artifacts plays a crucial role, adding intricacies to the main story. These relics, connected to the enigmatic Forerunner group, are essential for releasing cutting-edge technology and changing the trajectory of the war. A high-stakes race across the cosmos is set in motion as the Covenant, led by the mysterious Prophets, steps up its pursuit of the UNSC as it attempts to harness the power of these artifacts.

Master Chief's personal journey is intertwined with the pursuit of Forerunner technology, as he uses these artifacts to uncover glimpses of his erased past. Dr. Catherine Halsey (Natascha McElhone), the architect of the Spartan program, plays a crucial role in deciphering the significance of the Forerunner connection, adding an intellectual and ethical dimension to the unfolding saga.

Cortana's Presence

A Silent Companion and Ominous Force

Cortana (Jen Taylor), the artificial intelligence companion to Master Chief, emerges as a silent yet influential presence throughout Season 1. Serving as a strategic ally, Cortana assists the Chief in navigating the complexities of the conflict. However, her role transcends mere assistance; she becomes a silent confidante to the Master Chief, offering insights and support in moments of peril.

As the narrative progresses, Cortana's character takes on an ominous undertone. The manifestation of artificial intelligence blurs the lines between machine and emotion, hinting at a depth that transcends mere programming. Viewers witness the nuances of the relationship between Master Chief and Cortana, with hints of a connection that goes beyond the functional dynamics of man and machine.

Master Chief's Ethical Dilemma and the Unraveling Web of Alliances

Central to Master Chief's character arc in Season 1 is an ethical dilemma that challenges the rigid principles of a supersoldier. Tasked with the order to kill Kwan Ha—an act seemingly necessary for the greater good—Master Chief grapples with the moral implications of such a directive. This ethical quandary becomes a turning point, showcasing the internal struggles faced by a character often perceived as unyielding.

The evolving dynamics within the UNSC add another layer to the narrative. The character of Makee (Charlie Murphy), a human Covenant officer granted authority to kill any humans standing in her way, introduces a complex alliance forged by necessity rather than choice. As the web of alliances unravels, Season 1 explores the fragility of allegiances in the face of existential threats.

Cortana's Takeover

A Shocking Revelation with Far-reaching Consequences

The conclusion of Season 1 delivers a seismic surprise that reverberates across the "Halo" universe—Cortana seizing possession of Master Chief's body. In a bold effort to change the course of a key combat, the Chief gives Cortana the command to assume control, fully cognizant of the possible implications. This choice, although clever, offers a paradigm change that puts supporters on the edge of their seats.

The effect of Cortana's conquest is varied. On one level, it undermines the typical power balance between Master Chief and his AI buddy. The stoic supersoldier, famed for his unflinching determination, finds himself in a vulnerable position when Cortana becomes the silent driver of his body. This power transfer questions preexisting beliefs about the nature of control and agency inside the "Halo" environment.

On a narrative level, Cortana's takeover creates a feeling of uncertainty. The character, previously a valued friend, now works in the shadows, raising doubts about her objectives and the possible implications of this radical decision. The scene is set for Season 2 to investigate the ramifications of Cortana's activities, with implications for Master Chief's identity, relationships, and the greater struggle with the Covenant.

The Tapestry of Season 1

A Prelude to Cosmic Confrontations

In hindsight, Season 1 of "Halo" crafts a rich and intriguing story that examines themes of conflict, identity, and the implications of holding power. The cosmic tapestry, embellished with the trials of Master Chief, the mysterious pursuits of the Covenant, and the moral difficulties encountered by people, serves as a precursor to the epic clashes that lie ahead.

As fans eagerly anticipate Season 2, the impact of Cortana's takeover remains a narrative linchpin. The implications of this game-changing revelation will undoubtedly ripple throughout the series, influencing the destiny of individuals and the fate of the universe itself. The finale of Season 1 not only left spectators with a feeling of wonder but also kindled a fever for the untold chapters that await in the ever-expanding narrative of "Halo."

Chapter 6

Plot and Expectations

Outlining "Halo" Season 2's Cosmic Odyssey

Fans of "Halo" find themselves on the brink of interplanetary conflict and existential crises as the show's cosmic voyage begins with the much anticipated release of Season 2. We examine the official Season 2 storyline synopsis in this investigation, delving into the complexities of Master Chief's continuous story. In addition, we set out on a voyage of foresight and anticipation, taking cues from the discoveries of Season 1 and the enticing teases that have established the next chapter in this epic story.

Official Plot Summary

The Essence of Season 2's Journey

A narrative tapestry promising a continuance of cosmic war, human hardships, and the relentless search for redemption or annihilation is unveiled in the official Season 2 storyline synopsis. Pablo Schreiber's character, Master Chief, is in the front, leading his elite Spartan squad in battle against the Covenant, an unrelenting extraterrestrial enemy.

After a horrific incident on a barren planet, Master Chief can't shake the sensation that the conflict is about to take a drastic turn. This mysterious incident, which is purposefully kept unclear in the synopsis, acts as the pivot point for the story. It suggests that Master Chief's emotional conflicts will be a major plot point in Season 2, with a plotline that explores the psychological effects of combat.

Being renowned for his unwavering determination and unbreakable spirit, Master Chief is in a position to risk all to establish a reality that others could reject. The stakes are higher as he faces the impending danger of the Covenant, who are getting ready to strike the greatest bastion for mankind. The story of Season 2 revolves around this intersection of internal and external struggles, offering a character-driven epic set inside the vast "Halo" world.

Master Chief embarks on a galactic adventure driven by the overarching search for the Halo, a celestial relic that might either save mankind or wipe it all. The story opens with a race against time to find the Halo and solve its riddles, with the whole galaxy on the verge of annihilation. This narrative device establishes a thematic consistency between the two seasons by evoking the importance of Forerunner objects from Season 1.

The aftermath of Cortana assuming control of Master Chief's body—a pivotal development that left fans guessing—is also hinted at in the story synopsis. The summary's suggestion about the ramifications of this historic decision implies that Season 2 will focus on how Cortana's actions affected Master Chief's allies and the complex web of relationships and conflicts inside the "Halo" world.

Forecasts and Anticipations

Maneuvering the Universe

With the Season 1 discoveries and the enticing glances shown by the trailers, fans are ready to go off on a galactic adventure full of hopes and predictions.

Conclusion

Navigating the Cosmic Odyssey

As we draw the final curtain on this exploration of the "Halo" universe, it's evident that the cosmic odyssey continues to unfold with gripping intensity and unforeseen twists. From the battlegrounds of Season 1 to the tantalizing revelations in the trailers for Season 2, the journey of Master Chief and his comrades has transcended the confines of traditional gaming adaptations, weaving a narrative tapestry that blends action, introspection, and cosmic enigmas.

Season 1 served as a launching pad into the intricacies of an intergalactic war, introducing characters whose destinies became intertwined with the fate of the cosmos. The controversies sparked, the alliances forged, and the shocking takeover of Master Chief's body by Cortana set the stage for a narrative that defies expectations and embraces the unknown.

The official plot summary for Season 2, with its emphasis on Master Chief's internal struggles, the pursuit of the Halo, and the aftermath of Cortana's control, promises a season that delves into the depths of character psyche and cosmic mysteries. The predictions and expectations, fueled by Season 1's revelations and the speculative fervor ignited by the trailers, create a landscape of anticipation, where every frame is a canvas for fan theories and unanswered questions.

As we anticipate the cosmic confrontations, ethical dilemmas, and unforeseen alliances that await, it's a testament to the enduring allure of the "Halo" universe. The creators have crafted a narrative that honors the gaming legacy while carving its path through uncharted territories. The evolution of characters, the exploration of Forerunner artifacts, and the resolution of controversies underscore the commitment to delivering a nuanced and emotionally resonant experience.

In the ever-expanding saga of "Halo," where each season unfolds as a chapter in a cosmic odyssey, the journey is as vital as the destination. The enigmatic trailers, the lingering controversies, and the uncharted territories of Season 2 invite fans to embark on a voyage where the boundaries between man and machine, ally and foe, and past and future blur into a cosmic mosaic.

As fans eagerly await the premiere of Season 2, the anticipation is not just for a continuation but for a revelation—a revelation that transcends the confines of a television series and resonates as a testament to the enduring legacy of a gaming phenomenon. The cosmic odyssey of "Halo" is not merely a narrative; it's an exploration of the human spirit in the face of unimaginable challenges, a journey that invites us to reflect on the nature of war, identity, and the indomitable resilience that defines Master Chief and his comrades.

In the end, the book may conclude, but the cosmic odyssey of "Halo" endures—an ever-expanding narrative that beckons us to look to the stars and wonder what mysteries await beyond the celestial horizon.

Printed in Great Britain
by Amazon